I0105705

Perspectives of Nature
Selected Works

Perspectives of Nature Selected Works
ISBN (print book): 978-1-955762-12-0
ISBN (ebook): 978-1-955762-13-7

Copyright © 2024 by Paul Košir
First published 2024
sciromanticpoetry@gmail.com

With the exception of brief quotes for the purpose of review, no part of this book may be reproduced or utilized in any form or by any means, electronic or mechanical, without express written permission from the author.

Published by
The Shy Writer
www.theshywriter.org

Cover art by Lilly Košir, author's wife.
Taken at Yellowstone National Park
with sons, Owen and Brian, on the back cover

ACKNOWLEDGEMENTS

I must gratefully acknowledge
Rodney Schroeter,
whose confidence from the beginning
in my scientifically romantic style of poetry
made this project imaginable.

I also must gratefully acknowledge
the contributions to this work
by the members of our
Wednesday Night Poets Group,
who helped me polish my good poems
into publishable works.

Finally, I must gratefully acknowledge
my wife, Lilly, and our son, Owen,
for their cheerful and helpful responses
to my frequent questions and complaints
while dealing ineffectively
with computer situations.

Author's Introduction

In the late 1980s, when I was close to 30 years of age, I wrote about a dozen poems, all of which were "excellent" (my old high school English teacher's word, not mine). Critics agreed and "The Northern Lights" won third place in the Wisconsin Writers Association statewide Jade Ring Contest. That was all the encouragement I needed to embark upon my first collection of poetry, *Perspectives of Nature* and three more volumes of the same title. While writing the poems for the collections in this book, it was obvious that I already had my own style. But what to name it?

Romantic? Throughout my poems, Nature and Time have been capitalized, but not romanticized, researched, but not glorified, observed, but not interpreted. So not Romantic.

I ascribe much of what goes on in Nature as being done at the hand of Mother Nature or of Father Time, but these are devices of poetic license I have used to describe how animals and plants interact with their environment, but without romanticizing that interaction. No plants or animals ever conferred with Nature about their lot in life. Yet these very plants and animals engender personal feelings in the reader, which is a trademark of the Romantic Movement in poetry. So, my style is certainly Romantic, but still scientific.

Perhaps scientifically Romantic. Yes, that's my style Scientifically Romantic.

William Wordsworth, a founder of the Romantic Movement, said "poetry is the spontaneous overflow of powerful feelings." May you have many 'Wordsworthian' moments as you read the poetry in the selected works of the four volumes of *Perspectives of Nature.*

Many of the poems in this book use scientific terms. Definitions of more obscure terms and less-frequently-used words can be found on the left-hand pages opposite the poem in which the words or terms occur.

Readers may want to use the blank portions of the left-hand pages for journal entries, recording when and where events described in the poems are observed. Seeing a light pillar or the Milky Way, experiencing a mayfly hatch, or even finding a cowbird egg in a nest, are all worthy of journal entries. Writing in this book would not mar its pages, but cause them to flower.

The poems in this book were selected from the four volumes of *Perspectives of Nature* because they seemed to the author to be imaginative, creative, descriptive, thought-provoking, or had deep meaning.

Here, then, are the best poems of volumes one through four of *Perspectives of Nature plus ten new poems.*

- - - P. K.

To Owen,

who's always been the best son he could be.

Table of Contents

Acknowledgements............................ iii
Author's Introduction......................... iv
Dedication..................................... vii
Time... 1
Using Time..................................... 3
The Duel....................................... 5
Grasshopper Sparrow.......................... 7
Warblers....................................... 9
Feeding Bison.................................. 11
Life's History................................. 13
Color Blind.................................... 15
Hummingbird Trap............................. 17
The Northern Lights........................... 19
Leafcutter Ants................................ 21
Earth's Gems.................................. 23
Porcupine...................................... 25
Honey.. 27
Syrup.. 29
Birthday Presents............................. 31
Ferns.. 33
Prairie... 35
Heat... 37
Gooseberries................................... 39
Marsh.. 41
Turtle Shells................................... 43
Light... 45
Nettles... 47
Soil.. 49
Warmth... 51
First Bird Walk................................ 53
Fruits.. 55
Shelter... 57
Incredible Edibles............................. 59
Menu... 61
Killdeer.. 63

The Sighting.................................. 65
Erosion.. 67
Bird Song..................................... 69
Fireflies....................................... 71
Frog Call...................................... 73
Water.. 75
Crickets....................................... 77
Earth... 79
Parenting...................................... 81
Flying.. 83
Spider Webs.................................. 85
Tree Fall...................................... 87
Who Said I Didn't Go?..................... 89
A Surprise.................................... 91
Another Surprise............................ 93
* A Chance Encounter..................... 95
* Bullhead Fishing......................... 97
* A Moment With Grandma............... 99
* Jacob's Ladder........................... 101
* Maps....................................... 103
* Salamander............................... 105
* Natural History.......................... 107
Milky Way.................................... 109
Meteors....................................... 111
Eclipses....................................... 113
Sun... 115
Full Moons................................... 117
The Heavens................................. 119
* Musseltown............................... 121
* Two Tales of a Grasshopper............ 123
* Mr Saltzmann's Garden................. 125
About the Author............................ 127

*New poems are denoted with an * in front of the title*

TIME

The thread of Life rolls out in Spring
to near infinity,

and ties together living things
in Time's divinity.

Our Summer tablet holds a list, a simple registry
of tasks and fancies for our lives that we in mind foresee.

We turn the pages, ledger days against imagined Time,
our Summer stolen by a count not done by final chime.

At Autumn's feast on Winter's eve
Time cools in hibernation

while other patrons quickly eat,
Time warms in their migration.

How long, it seems, the Winter lasts
as marked by Winter Wren,

count seven seconds for each song
that's absent from his glen.

Notes

USING TIME

The never-ending currency
of Time well-spent today

will ne'er be lost, but always found,
whatever come what may.

Struck only once by hands of Time,
but minted every day

and crafted into food and drink,
exchanging weigh for whey.

Our recompense for daily toil
is promise of more work,

until we cease our labors there
our duties for to shirk.

The gold we've sought through our careers
cannot be held in hand,

but choices that at last we make
based solely on the Land.

Notes

THE DUEL

So pleasant was the evening air and moonlit were the skies,
the crickets in the distance chirped, sweet fragrance on the rise.

The pipes were clogged, I washed by hand the night we had our duel.
I only wanted dishes clean and never to be cruel.

The wind picked up and rustled leaves, light rain began to fall,
an owl let out a warning hoot, and darkness cast a pall.

I washed the dishes, one by one, then put them in a rack,
next, took the dishpan through the house to empty from the back.

There was a sound, some feet away; I wondered what it was
because I know night noises not as well as Nature does.

I heaved the water anyway, but acted as a fool;
my toss became initial shot in very short-lived duel.

I saw no beast until it turned, then black back showed stripe white.
The skunk did not with rancor aim, yet squirted me with might.

Notes

Bucolic *("byu-KAH-lick")*
   Pastoral, rural.

Heifers *("heff-erz")*
   Young female bovines that have not yet calved.
   (Cows already have calved.)

GRASSHOPPER SPARROW

My dad grew up on sandy farm in center of our state,
bucolic lessons in his heart, experiences great

truck farming spuds and roofing barns with ice cream as a goal.
He'd beat the heat, once chores were done, down at the swimming hole.

His lessons in biology were making heifers cows.
'Tween shearing sheep, he learned the birds, who sang while sheep would browse.

It always seemed he knew the birds and mammals that we saw.

With mentor set, my goal was clear – learn birds without a flaw.

One day he pointed in the sky, said "nighthawk" with a smile.
"How do you know? What makes it so?" He said, "I guess, its style."

Not learning from his farm-taught ways, I gave to them a pass.
Instead, I thought, while off at school, I'd take a birding class.

In May one year, while home from school, we visited a park.
I wished to show him birds I'd learned, like cuckoos and a lark.

When we saw jays and chickadees, my dad was in his prime,
but warblers, thrushes, vireos would fool him every time.

Most birds we saw were new to him, I didn't want to chide,
but finished with a bird ID that might have hurt his pride.

When something buzzed, my father said, relief upon his face,
"At least I know what made that sound – grasshopper in this place."

I knew the call, we whirled around to see the birding treat,
Grasshopper *sparrow* on a stump, my triumph bittersweet.

Notes

WARBLERS

They never stop moving, I can't get a good look;
when they finally sit perched, it's not like in the book.

All seem to be yellow and they look just the same,
so the hardest thing yet is to call each by name.

And their warbling songs are no treat to my ears;
the sneaks hide behind leaves then taunt me with jeers.

I'll look in the tree tops, that's the best place to check;
that'll prove that all warblers are a pain in the neck!

Notes

*This poem is from a different era.
It is not wise, nor encouraged to get close to bison.
Do not try to feed them, nor touch them.*

FEEDING BISON

The herd was tens of millions strong when money changed no hands,

yet currency of bison skins brought more and more demands.

Once ev'rywhere but near the coasts, no thought they'd disappear,

Then slaughter inconceivable, two million in a year.

Two dozen left in Yellowstone created public fears.

No longer being targeted helped dry the public's tears.

Restrictive hunting laws enforced, the bison bred like deer.

Now herd is half-a-million head, their comeback makes us cheer.

We drove all day on family trip in station wagon car;

no phones or tunes or videos, the drive seemed very far.

We missed by minutes open hours to see the bison park,

With silver tongue, Dad made a deal that wouldn't miss the mark.

We'd ride along with staff and feed the bison herd a snack

with Mom in middle, Dad on right, and children in the back.

A worker drove us in his truck to middle of the herd.

"Don't touch the horns!" he sternly warned two times and then a third.

Its head as big as all of me, I feared for being bit,

but there, inside the pickup truck, I didn't want to quit.

Such herbivores ate only grass, so it would do no harm.

Yet when I fed it pellet food, it sucked up half my arm.

*N*otes

Punctuations
    Periods of geologically rapid evolutionary change.

Sedimentation
    Deposited minerals that become rock and organic material
    that becomes fossils.

LIFE'S HISTORY

The hardest things in Life are ne'er forgotten,
they're set for the ages and written in stone:

the strength that suffuses a primitive shell,
the framework supporting Life cut to the bone

are clues to the mysteries unfolded in Life,
posterity left in impressions of yore,

punctuations engraved in layers of rock,
a record of Life as it's lived at its core.

Yet daily existence and struggles in life,
actions and instincts in Nature's creation,

learning in offspring and tending by parents
occur without trace in sedimentation.

Earth publishes not what living things utter,
their unnoted thoughts are forgotten and dead.

The soft parts of Life are all in the Present,
imbued with their genes for the Future ahead.

Notes

Espial *("ess-PILE")*
  Espying, catching sight of.

COLOR BLIND

With man-made hues, I'm color blind; I do not know the tints
of fabrics in the fashion world or tinctures found in chintz.

I know not French nor heraldry, so not the color vert.
What I see best are Nature's tones and different shades of dirt.

Some tinges that I do not know are taupe and puce and dun;
they're artificial stylish dyes, made indoors, not in sun.

Sienna brown, I never know, if yellowish or red.
Cerise is red that's light and clear whenever it is said.

Not so for "lake," a word for red that means deep water blue
or "madder," yellow-flowered plant, that's also reddish hue.

And "fallow" means a resting field, but also yellow shade;
I've seen this color many times, as fields begin to fade.

Cerulean is blue I know, a warbler streaked on back.
A bunting male looks indigo yet pigment only black.

I see the light, reflected blue; it always makes me smile:
not color-blind, I see what's hid – the bunting blue espial.

Notes

HUMMINGBIRD TRAP

The smallest bird I'd ever seen, its back and wings metallic green,

ensnared within a monstrous trap with, at one end, enormous gap,

held hostage by the thought ingrained that flying up is freedom gained.

Without delay and not a word, I raised a staff to help the bird.

On end it perched repeatedly, I dipped the pole to set it free.

Each time it got near open space, it flew to roof-board closed-in place.

The hummingbird began to fade, once buzzing past, it now was staid.

The little bird had little time; with bag in hand, I made my climb.

Ascending to within arm's length, I saw the hummer losing strength.

I slowly reached out with my hand to catch what now could barely stand.

Through porous bones I felt its heart, its tiny, racing, living part.

With lightest touch, I held the life that on each front found danger rife.

I gently placed it in the sack, crawled 'round the rafter beam and back

to shaky ladder down I crept while female ruby-throated slept.

When finally down upon the Earth, I ope'd the pouch and gave rebirth.

It flew to food, red blossoms fair, and from garage, the man-made snare.

Notes

Ion *("EYE-on")*
    An atom or group of atoms that has lost or gained one or more electrons.

Empyreal *("em-PURR-ee-ul")*
    Relating to the visible heavens.

Solar flare
    A short-lived outburst of solar material releasing enormous amounts of energy.

Aurora Boreal *("aw-ROAR-uh BORE-ee-ul")*
    Aurora Borealis, the Northern Lights.

THE NORTHERN LIGHTS

When God, in Mother Nature's guise,
sheds Her grace upon the skies,

She magnetizes ions aerial,
preparing firmament empyreal

so that each lofty atom shines
along the Earth's magnetic lines,

in pulsing, starlit choreography,
handwritten there in bright calligraphy.

While brushing hues above the air
by virtue of a solar flare,

She weaves Her light rays into tapestry,
unveiling meteoric artistry

by drawing draperies of light
across the northern polar night,

illuminating skies ethereal,
aglow with rare Aurora Boreal.

Notes

Caste
   A grouping of social insects all of which
   have the same function in the colony.

High Hopes
   The 1959 song made popular by
   Frank Sinatra about attempts by an ant
   to move a rubber tree plant.

LEAFCUTTER ANTS

Some thousands of chambers for queen and her kin,
but only her daughters will live there within.

From dozens to millions, a colony holds
the ants for all jobs in production of molds:

Cut leaves while they're green, store in beds underground,
make mulch for the fungus to which they are bound.

The labor's divided by size for each caste,
the soldiers are largest, while farmers are last.

Crop-growers, as smallest, take care of the young;
they vaccinate larvae and take out the dung

The larger ants sometimes will help clear a trail
if an object's too big and smaller ants fail

With leaf-cutting roles so ingrained in the ants,
they'll never be movers of rubber tree plants,

but slippery leaves with which no insect copes,
mean ant could not move them, whatever her hopes.

Chalcedony *("kal-SED-oh-nee")*
  A form of quartz.

Saturated
  As much of a substance dissolved as possible.

Solutes *("SAHL-yutes")*
  The substances being dissolved.

Ovoid
  Egg-shaped.

Moganite
  Mineral that forms around agates.

Silica = silicon dioxide (SiO_2)
  Common mineral that can be of different colors, depending on the impurities present.

Nucleation points *("new-klee-AY-shun)*
  Points of origination for coloration.

EARTH'S GEMS

Geodes

In secret, Nature lays her eggs, rocks lacking artistry;
no decorations on their shells of quartz chalcedony.

Instead, their shells, when broken, show the mineral gifts inside,
from solutions saturated, there grew solutes that since dried.

A crystal palace lies within each dingy ovoid stone;
amid the gems, a seat unseen for Mother Nature's throne.

Each floor and wall with jewels bedecked, on ceilings, chandeliers.
The other geodes, still intact, unopened through the years.

Agates

As gases of the early Earth escaped its lava flows,
then Time made cooling bubble frames and fashioned studios

with outer walls of moganite, which looked like normal stones,
but inside, workshops stocked with gel-like silica for tones

to paint small frescoes on the walls at nucleation points,
adhering there with micro-crystal curvy fiber joints.

More coats, more coats till Time is done; the agate filled, unique.
When hewn, it shows the banding that the agate-hunters seek.

Notes

Crepuscular
Active in the twilight hours of dawn and dusk.

Hiawatha
The Hiawatha *(high-uh-WAH-thuh)* National
Forest is in the Upper Peninsula of Michigan.

PORCUPINE

Each year we count our breeding birds
to note the rise or fall

of numbers in their habitats
and help when they get small.

To Hiawatha first we went,
where counters were before,

to chart how data changed from past,
the science not a chore.

Arising much more difficult
at quarter after four.

Then we saw life crepuscular,
a porcupine afore.

I rushed to pet the animal,
just missed the needled beast.

I tried to show bravado,
but pet attempt was least.

*N*otes

Forage bees
    The bees that forage for nectar, pollen, and water.

Enzyme
    A protein acting as a catalyst in a biochemical reaction.

Hexagon-al
    Six sided

Royal Jelly
    Secretion from that is fed to the queen and all young bees.

Drones
    Male bees that do no work and have the sole purpose of
    mating with the queen.

HONEY

I pet a bee whene'er I dare, I try not to recoil,
for in this clumsy way I try to thank her for her toil.

I watch the workers, one by one, across the meadow fly;
the forage bees have said with dance that there the flowers lie.

Some flowers' petals guide the bees and show them where to light
to gather nectar from each bloom, and pollen, dry and bright.

With baskets full of pollen food, they make a bee-line back,
the nectar sipped by worker bees still held in special sac.

By work of mouth an enzyme turns the nectar each bee brings,
to honey thin that next is fanned as workers flap their wings.

The thickened sweet is stored in combs of hexagon-al cells
and capped with wax for winter food, creating honey wells.

The royal jelly's made and fed three days to all young bees,
but on and on to larvae crowned "queen mother," if you please.

By mating with the male drones, establishing her brood,
she gives them life, then I can share their produce and their food.

Phloem *("FLOW-em")*
    The vascular tissue that conducts the sugars
    and other products of photosynthesis from the
    leaves to the roots of plants.

Xylem *("ZYE-lem")*
    The vascular tissue that conducts water and some
    nutrients from the roots to the stems and leaves of plants.

SYRUP

While frosty morns are warmed by day
and sunny days at night turn cold,
the life of trees begins to flow
and maples pump their liquid gold.

A year before, their leaves did catch
the strength of Sun, the breath of air
to fuel the trees' life-giving sap,
stored underground for Winter bare.

Descended through the phloem tubes
in Summer's growth and Autumn's fall,
life rested Winter under snow,
rising back through xylem tall.

In early Spring, when frozen trees
begin to thaw in mildest heat,
some tap the flowing life dilute,
distilling from it something sweet.

Notes

Dapple
   Become marked with rounded
   patches of color or light.

Troll
   Fish from a slowly moving boat
   or other craft.

Ice floe
   A floating chunk of ice in a river

BIRTHDAY PRESENTS

My wife enjoys her birthday date,
it always falls in March.

She never asks for birthday cake
with sweeteners or starch.

She likes instead to go outside,
clear weather, rain, or snow

to dapple in the sunny spots
along the river's flow.

Her greatest thrill is eagles seen,
in air, on ice, or nest,

or trolling from an ice floe chunk
that gives birds' wings a rest.

This burst of Life at Winter's close,
when eagles congregate,

one hundred thirty numbered once
and made her celebrate.

Notes

18.5 Fern species
   The two fern species highlighted in this poem
   are the Bulblet Fern and the Walking Fern.

Strown
   (Past participle of strow,
   the archaic form of strew.)
   Scattered or spread about.

FERNS

I took a stroll on shady bluff between two types of ferns,
while one could follow any path, one only downward turns.

Each species reproduced itself by spores and not by seeds,
so cloaked the cliff with lacy green, not flower-colored weeds.

Though tiny, spores hold DNA instructions for each plant,
spores moist and sheltered, germinate, but otherwise they can't.

Two generations alternate, the "fern", or sporophyte,
and overlooked gametophyte, a fingernail in height.

The ferns along the trail I trod regenerated there,
without the spores of other ferns nor reproductive pair.

Ferns do it vegetatively, each bulb is then a clone,
a tiny bulb along plant's keel, by Mother Nature strown.

Dried bulblets move by gravity, along the bluff-side edge
until they meet an obstacle, stopped by a little ledge.

The other fern can 'walk' the Earth, re-rooting forms its 'grip',
then takes a step, a growing stride, re-roots again at tip.

Notes

Seres *(sears)*
   Stages in secondary ecological succession,
   which occurs after an area is invaded by plants.

PRAIRIE

Sedges have edges and rushes are round,
but grasses are hollow from top to the ground.

First two like wetness, but grasses not so;
they're native to Plains states, where winds often blow,

growing in grasslands called prairies by name;
the rich soils beneath them made landscapes to tame.

Prairies remain on the lands undisturbed,
but only in places where plowing was curbed.

Flames on the prairie, ignited with ease,
burn all the dead grasses and smallest of trees,

properly managed and set through the years,
they guided succession in stages, or seres.

Grassland savannahs have trees of great girth,
with deep-growing roots that help anchor the Earth.

Climax of plant life may not be the trees,
but grasses and flowers in warm Summer breeze.

*N*otes

Caloric
  The fluid that transferred heat according to the obsolete "caloric theory" from the middle to the end of the 19th century.

Kinetic
  Related to or explained by motion.

HEAT

Before the nineteenth century, "caloric" carried heat
in scientific papers and while walking down the street.

This liquid explanation of how warm things got warm
became replaced by energy, kinetic in its form.

Kinetic heat is passed along in one way out of three:
conduction, radiation, and convection we can see.

Conduction must by contact spread from warmer to the cool,
Warm things, when felt, start losing heat; this state can sometimes fool.

Convective heat by currents moves, in rooms and Gulf and core.
Heat rises to the ceiling, so it's cooler near the floor.

The Gulf Stream carries water to the European states,
which makes them warm for folks to live and betters, then, their fates.

Currents in its outer core cause Earth's magnetic field
that saves us from Sun's cosmic rays, without it, fate is sealed.

By radiation, heat is passed to objects far away,
thus Ultraviolet energy is carried by Sun's ray

then through transparent barriers, including greenhouse glass,
and CO_2 or methane or some other greenhouse gas.

These U-V rays are turned to heat that's trapped below the sky
to warm the Earth and make some think disaster's coming nigh.

Notes

Many gooseberry (*Ribes*) species have no prickles
on the berry, but the shrub in our yard was *Ribes cynosbati*,
called prickly gooseberry or dogberry, which had them.

GOOSEBERRIES

One day while swinging happily, when I was just a lad,
I heard him call from 'cross the lawn, so ran to be with Dad.

"They're ready, Son," he smiled at me. I peered around his knee
then stared in horror at the shrub, "There's prickers!" was my plea.

Dad said the berries tasted good and gave me some to try.
I paused and backed a step or two and then began to cry.

I whined and whimpered endlessly; I did not want to eat
the pea-sized fruits with pointy parts, though Dad called them a treat.

He said again they would not hurt; my heart and mind were torn.
He ate a few to prove them safe, I touched the longest thorn.

"The fresh new spines are soft, not sharp," said Dad's assuring voice.
I sniffled once then wiped my tears, looked up and made my choice.

The unripe fruits had tasty crunch, two acids made them tart.
Dad always knew I'd say someday, "I loved them from the start."

*N*otes

This poem was inspired by the La Crosse River Marsh,
a 1200-acre wetland in the middle of La Crosse, Wisconsin.

MARSH

A bur-reed marsh is mostly there,
where cat-tail plants are somewhat rare.

While threatened species fly around,
invasive species grow from ground.

Marsh dried a Mississippi flood
to make it Mississippi mud

in the year, Two Thousand One
and '50s, '60s, still not done.

Teachers use for education,
others find their recreation,

A place where scholars do research,
and spirits treat it as a church.

Blackbird, egret, dragonfly,
a wood duck painted on the sky,

fishes, muskrats swimming past,
gosling follows mama last,

swallow, warbler, leopard frog,
turtles sunning on a log.

All these things seen in "The Marsh,"
where Summer's gentle, Winter's harsh.

Notes

Scutes *(skoots)* or *(skyoots)*
   Horny or boney plates covering a turtle's shell.

TURTLE SHELLS

A turtle with no shell attached would not a turtle be.
Its shell encumbers not its life, but neither sets it free.
Protective plates upon its back, reduced mobility,
adaptation set the course for shell anatomy

Its scutes as plates of armor serve to shield and thus defend
both body and the skin beneath, on which the scutes depend.

The upper shell, or carapace, makes turtles look distinct
while plastron, or the lower shell, by flesh and bone is linked.

Box turtle species have a "hinge" across the bottom shell
affording them a little "box" in which they fit quite well.

By pulling in all legs and head. they hide from predators,
then pressing plastron, carapace, will open up its "doors."

The Blanding's turtle (semi-box) has "hinge" that's used in fear
to cover head and legs in front, but not the ones in rear

An adaptation found in some freshwater-dwelling kinds
is soft shell with consistency of firmest citrus rinds.

The Swinhoe's softshell, rare on the Earth can live a hundred years,
so nearly all were hunted out, now real extinction nears.
A male lives in captivity, a female, Viet Nam.
These two must be together bred so she can be a mom.

Planar
    In a flat plane.

Obliquities *(oh-BLICK-wi-tees)*
    Deviations from a right line or flat plane.

Convex
    For lenses, thicker in the center.

Concave
    For lenses, thinner in the center.

Angle of incidence
    Angle at which light enters a mirror, lens, or prism.

Newton = Sir Isaac Newton (1642-1727)
    English physicist and mathematician.

Whit
    A particle of the least possible amount.

LIGHT

To the looking glass and back, describes the path of light,
reflected from its silvered rear, that's polished clean and bright.
The image seen is regular, transposed from left to right.
What else has turned to wonderland in image of our sight?

By moving to another glass, we change reflected view,
the mirror now not planar, so its image is askew,
which alters our perspective so it's something wholly new,
removing the obliquities that quite unnoticed grew.

But through the looking lens and on, will cause a bended ray.
An arrow 'hind a water glass will point the other way.
The shape of lens, convex, concave, decides how it will stray
from angle of its incidence, where it will rarely stay.

With mirrors and a lens inside, he built a viewing tool
to help his students learn at night in most impressive school.
As Newton worked, invented math, new physics, as a rule,
he looked at planets' orbits while he sat upon on his stool.

Through the prism and beyond, is where white light is split,
revealing spectrum locked within, six colors to be lit.
The rainbow's seen at other times, in water spray, oil bit.
Light's nature is duality, part wavy and part whit.

Notes

NETTLES

One day while at the garden bed, when I was just a child,
my father tried to teach me weeds encroaching from the wild.

"Come over, Son, and feel this plant, with nettle for a name."
My tender fingers burned and itched, as if too near a flame.

Much later, while a nature guide, I studied nettle plants,
which have the formic acid found in painful biting ants.

The hollow hairs of stem and leaf break off and then inject
their acid into skin laid bare, where clothes do not protect.

Laportea, wood-nettle, grows in shaded, wooded stands,
but stinging nettles, *Urtica*, in open, vacant lands.

With cooking, nettles lose their sting, are safe and edible.
Their simmered leaves and cooking broth each taste incredible.

While leading hikes, I always warned to touch no nettles raw,
nor eat them without cooking first, lest feel a throbbing maw.

One day while hiking on his trails, I told this to my dad,
who bested me a second time, ate nettles and was glad.

Profile
   The arrangement of the constituent horizontal layers of soil.

Horizons
   The various identifiable layers: O, A, E, B, C,
   and sometimes R (rock) that make up soil.

SOIL

The bedrock of an area is parent rock of soil,
produced by Nature and by Time, no touch of human toil.

Rock broken by the freeze-and-thaw of water on the land
shaped mineral ingredients, like clay and silt and sand.

By color, texture, structure can a soil be classified;
in profile and horizons, can development be spied.

Material from Life on Earth, organic in its source,
imparts the chemistry of Life, but not the living force.

Such matter and some broken rock are all soil needs to form,
then sculpted by the climate and by weather, sun or storm.

Organic matter, decomposed, is food for plants to grow,
if in a place by Nature set, or planted in a row,

eroded soil is gone for good, take care of where we 'tread.'
Formation takes a thousand years, so soil is limited.

Protect the soil and use it well, do not the landscape hurt.
Remember that our gift from Time, our soil, is more than dirt.

*N*otes

Metabolic heat
  The heat resulting from the biochemical
  reactions of life, animal heat.

WARMTH

In Autumn, shorter, cooler days
stir changes in the eating ways

of mammals who must often eat
to warm with metabolic heat.

While some continue on this road,
the finding-food-when-hungry mode,

a never-ending way of life
of feasting mixed with starving strife,

some species burrow underground
and wait for Spring to come around.

Some of the bats and many birds,
a butterfly and hoof-ed herds

migrate to find the better climes
to spend their hungry winter times.

As mammals, humans do the same.
As spirits, humans need a flame,

which friends and family help to light
to keep away the cold at night.

Some people hibernate or fly
to keep their bodies warm and dry,

but miss the visits, kith and kin,
the chance to feel, to talk and grin.

Yes, Autumn is the time of year
to build up warmth and gather cheer.

Notes

FIRST BIRD WALK

I poorly planned my nature walk for first day in the park,
we watched the birds along the bluff, but hike soon left the mark.

Each step became more treacherous, no longer on the trail,
my leadership had showed us naught, but Nature did not fail.

Some dripping water showered birds, one green with yellow breast,
the other bird less camouflaged, with striking colors blest.

The red and black of male distinct, their contrast weakens knees,
but female held to different scale, her subtler colors please.

The male began the toileting, alighting rather low,
adjusting his positioning to dip beneath the flow.

Clear water splashed upon his head to make his body clean,
he perched upon a nearby twig and thereupon to preen.

The female scarlet tanager, at basin after mate,
used her time to cleanse her skin and comb her feathers straight.

Each sat before the fountain drips and took a final turn
then followed Nature, formed a bond, eloped behind a fern.

*N*otes

Moot
   Open to discussion, but of no significance.

Generatve
   Growing into a new plant, as, the fruits.

FRUITS

It cannot be, you must be wrong!
I'll show you books. It won't take long.

It sounds not right. How can it be?
Come take a look. Let's have a see.

That's not the story I've been told.
As scientists, we must be bold.

The question is no longer moot?
Tomatoes are a type of fruit!

Is it the only food like that?
When fruit puts on a veggie's hat?

And takes the culinary name?
even when it's not the same?

So many fruits from ovaries,
like peppers, olives, okra, peas,

still considered vegetative,
even though parts generative.

What rhubarb parts meet baking goals?
The stalks of leaves, or petioles.

Whatever fruity taste belief?
Not fruit, but stems of each large leaf.

Replaces fruit by those who bake,
and pinch off buds to crumbles make.

This sour produce just may be
what goes down hard **for you and me.**

Notes

CCC (Civilian Conservation Corps).
   A government program which, along with
   The Works Progress Administration (WPA)
   provided work for young men during the
   1930s at work camps like the one in Wyalusing.

Caterpillar® tread
   Tread of large earth-moving equipment.

Scutes *(skoots)* or *(skyoots)*
   Horny or boney plates covering a turtle's shell.

SHELTER

With our country at its poorest,
some young men made it rich;

they built us timeless treasures while
in governmental hitch.

In Wyalusing, shelters rose
at hands of CCC.

Though built for humans, used by bats,
without an entrance fee.

Bats congregate 'neath roofing boards
and squeak like mice on high.

They face adapted predator
that doesn't even fly.

A black rat snake can use its scutes
as Caterpillar® tread

to climb the rough-hewn timbers where
on bats itself is fed.

Notes

INCREDIBLE EDIBLES

One year while working at the park, I did a cooking show.
The weekly program was a hit, once filled up every row.

With forty to one hundred guests, I had to move with haste
to serve each one in audience a little sip or taste.

The food I served I cooked that night or in preceding week.
Before the meal we'd take a hike, more edibles to seek.

One night a man at table last, refused to eat the nettles.
He'd seen all other groupings eat the nettles dish from kettles.

He'd even watched his family eat and say to him, "Great, Dad."
But still refused… Then ate a dab. He grudged to say, "Not bad."

Another night, when show was done, a couple came, was glad.
When you said nettles had the taste that spinach also had,
we worried that our son would balk, for spinach was a pain.
He loved the nettles best of all, we really can't explain.
I spoke to them, behind my hand, Here's your new spinach plan.
Next time there's spinach on his plate, say, "Nettles from the can."

Notes

MENU

Tossed salad of edible greens
Soup: Dandelion broth
Appetizer: Morel mushrooms (from freezer)
Entrée: Nettles Italiano
Dessert: Wild ginger candy or
   Berry flummery (by season)
Beverage: Nettle tea

(Adapted from *Billy Joe Tatum's Wild Foods Field Guide and Cookbook*)

Notes

Ruse *(rooz)*
    A stratagem or trick.

Feign *(fane)*
    To pretend to be affected by something.

Ploy
    A stratagem or cunning maneuver.

Coy
    Shy, retiring, or pretending to be same.

Plover *(PLUH - ver or PLOH - ver)*
    A small wading bird.

Fits and starts
    Bit by bit.

Apportioning
    Dividing out into portions.

KILLDEER

While jogging 'long the Oakwood Road, a rural city street
in the County of Milwaukee, where Nature, suburb meet,

I saw a bird just sitting there, in shoulder of the lane.
It sat until I got too near and triggered ruse to feign.

With open nest upon the ground, it made a daring ploy,
it limped away with 'broken' wing, behavior never coy.

It led me as a 'predator' with thoughts of easy meal
until the plover flew away, squawked "killdeer," then, with zeal.

Rejuvenated from its 'wound,' it ran in fits and starts
Apportioning its getaway in many shorter parts

The next day, for my morning jog, I chose the other way
To give protective parent rest while at its nest could stay.

I looked not back, for I had seen behavior at its best,
to guard the eggs or nestlings that were camouflaged like nest.

I knew I'd miss the chance to see that bird repeat its trick,
But rather give best chance at life to each and every chick.

Notes

THE SIGHTING

An owl appeared and glided to a river bottom tree
and landed on the outer edge, a place that I could see.

It held its branch and looked for food upon the forest floor.
My view so good, the sight so rare, I watched a little more.

There were two tufts atop its head, but not where ears did grow;
they're buried deep in facial discs, one higher up, one low.

Such ears allow an owl at night to find whate'er it hears,
including noises under snow, and by those sounds it steers.

As well as sound, the facial discs can gather in scant light,
perceived by oddly-shaped large eyes as something almost bright.

Its eyes so big, they cannot move, an owl must turn its head,
from part-way rear and side to side, three-fourths around the spread.

With special fringing on its wings, an owl flies silently,
which helps it sneak up on its prey and kill it instantly.

Its perfect camouflage can help an owl avoid a stare.
The owl appeared and glided in, but then it wasn't there.

Notes

Ablate
  Wasting away or erosion of a glacier,
  iceberg, or rock by the melting of ice
  or the action of water.

Canyon Grand
  the Grand Canyon in Arizona.

Arches
  Arches National Park in Utah.

EROSION

With a steady, infinitesimal gait,

Time does all His work at a slow, even rate.

The persistence of Time will never abate,

even when frozen, will the surface ablate.

Time-honored erosion, need not mediate,

the work is unending, to disintegrate.

Time sharpens His tools for eroding the Land,

but tools in His kit are not built for the hand.

They have not a case nor an imprint nor brand.

With wind and some water, He beats earth to sand.

In two blinks of His eye, He dug Canyon Grand,

honed parabola Arches in rusty red band.

Notes

Henslow's
  Henslow's sparrow.

Syrinx *("SEAR-inks")*
  The vocal organ of birds, located at the fork of
  the trachea (windpipe).

BIRD SONG

In order to communicate, birds utter different calls,
a lexicon of notes in life as told through phonic scrawls.

Their sweeter songs have other goals; each male sings in his realm,
to shoo the other males away, woo females from the helm.

Her response to avian ads will carry on her race,
yet in her choice, she may begin a dialect of place.

The lyrics of each species, song are sung distinctively;
while judging features of each song, she rates him on his plea.

The longest and most intricate from tiny winter wren,
just a hiccup from the Henslow's as he wobbles to his den.

Most curious from bobolink – the oingo boingo bird –
yet even more unusual when two at once are heard.

A thrush sings with both syrinx sides, a different pitch in each,
making flute-like and ethereal the lonesome male's beseech.

These mimic thrushes copy snips from songs of other birds
grey catbirds once, brown thrashers twice, and mockingbirds do thirds.

More than a song from sandhill cranes, their courtship is a dance:
males rub on mud then bugle mates to intimately prance.

✍otes

Tracheoles *("TRAKE-ee-oles")*
  Fine tubes in insects that allow gas exchange.

Photuris
  A genus of fireflies.

FIREFLIES

When fireflies feel mating urge, males head to humid field
to cruise low vegetation haunts and signal lanterns wield.

Within these lamps, the chemicals react in mystery;
luciferin, luciferase make eerie light we see.

It's yellow, green, light red, or orange, one species even blue.
These magic 'flies withhold their light till dimness is their cue.

Then oxygen in tracheoles is fuel for bright, cool light;
without O2, reaction stops and 'flies blend in with night.

The bits of light are flashed by males, in pattern of their kind;
in Smoky Mountains, unison, in Rockies, dark 'flies find.

When ladies of the lightning bugs see gents with finest glow,
they wink assent by flashing lights that match the male's show.

The femme fatale *Photuris* 'bug fools males of other kinds
by mimicking their blinking codes to eat lured 'bugs she finds.

Pairs trip the light fantastic while at Nature's bug-lit ball;
their messages mean naught to us, yet still they do enthrall.

*N*otes

Anurans *("ah-NER-anz")*
   Frog and toad species.

Frog species appear in the poem in the order in which
they generally sing in Wisconsin and the Upper Midwest.

FROG CALLS

In springtime, frogs begin to call, in ponds and wetter lands.
Before each call, their lungs inhale, their vocal sac expands.

This air is forced from sac to lungs, but never is it breathed.
The frog or toad tight lipped remains, its tongue is ever sheathed.

When air flows o'er their vocal chords, anurans sing the songs
comprising aural signatures, distinct from that of throngs.

The calls establish breeding grounds, the songs attract new mates;
frogs in a chorus pattern sing to see how each male rates.

The competition orderly, one frog and then the next;
each solo artist sings his song, described in coming text.

A Wood Frog makes a croak from home
While Chorus Frogs strum on a comb.
The Peepers' peeps are next to spring,
And sound like distant sleighbells' ring.
A Leopard Frog rubs tight balloon,
a Pickerel then snores in tune.
For many seconds trills a Toad,
before Gray Treefrog's razzing flowed.
then Cope's Gray Treefrog buzzes back,
as Cricket Frogs two marbles clack.
The Mink Frog trots on cobblestone
and Green Frog twangs loose banjo tone.
The last anuran call from lake
is foghorn sound that Bullfrogs make.

*N*otes

Aqueous *("AY-kwi-us")*
   Taking place in or with water

Capillarity *("cap-ill-AIR-i-tee")*
   The tendency in narrow tubes for liquids to rise or
   fall by surface tension

Vascular *("VASS-cue-lahr")*
   A plant having cells specializing in moving water

Adhesion *("add-HEE-zhun")*
   The tendency of water to cling to other substances

Cohesion *("co-HEE-zhun")*
   The tendency of water to cling to itself

WATER

Unique among the molecules of compounds world around,
in liquid, gas, and solid states can water e'er be found.

All living things need H_2O, the chemical of life,
to bathe reactions aqueous, assuaging thirsting strife.

Yet Life itself depends on traits of water physical,
to help create and guide the surge of life force mystical.

Fresh water moves in lower plants by capillarity,
but vascular in higher plants, a flower or a tree.

Adhesion and cohesion move fresh water through each plant,
to transport Life's elixir to the places where it's scant.

And water shaped the faunal life that dwelt in ancient bays,
archaic fish developed gills, employing water's ways.

To fish that live in waters fresh, dissolved O_2 gives breath,
the floating ice and flow below allow for cheating death.

Cold water holds more oxygen, the life-sustaining gas,
so deeper in a frozen lake is where you'll find the bass.

Notes

Stridulate *(STRIJ-yu-late)*
   Of an insect, rubbing two body parts together to make
   a shrill, grating noise.

Perps
   Perpetrators of crimes such as unlawful entry.

Dynasty of Tang
   Rulers of the Chinese Empire from 618-907 who kept
   crickets in cages and venerated them.

CRICKETS

When male crickets want to mate,
they rub their wings and stridulate
by scraping 'scraper' 'cross their 'file'
a nearby female to beguile
with buzzy chirps in charming song,
again, again, the whole night long.
Most people find that crickets soothe
but others wish harsh chirping smooth.
Cave crickets, "mute," of wings devoid,
make some with basements feel annoyed.
Crickets chirp from planting rows
till harvest days come to a close
These bookends make the cricket sage
to those who shrine them in a cage.
At times in Western countries, jeered,
throughout the East, they are revered
for all the chirping songs they sang
from time of Dynasty of Tang.
Where crickets dwelt, good fortune found,
but here all live upon the ground.
Inside, a cricket stops its chirps
to signify invading perps.
Outside, crickets get a feel
for temp'ratures they then reveal.

*N*otes

Sentience *(SEN-tee-ens)*
Perception by the senses.

Corporeal *("CORE-pore-EE-ul")*
Relating to the bodily or physical realm.

EARTH

Inside my Mother Earth, I feel my senses go away:
no sight, no sound, no touch, no taste; my sentience does not stay.
As I descend, the light grows dim, my sight begins to gray
till blackness strikes my eyes so deep, there's nothing where I lay.
The sounds of life above persist, but not so where I rest;
the chamber walls are silent, in their stillness I am blest.
The air beyond turns still below, within my Mother's breast;
while sheltered here, I fail to feel my limbs that once were stressed.
Through muted lips do I perceive no sweet, no salt, no sour;
the only taste is bitterness of food from my last hour.
No longer can my nose provide the fragrance of a flower,
for scent is barely issued from these walls severe and dour.
The vault that holds my earthly self is not for me a grave.
Immobile, not inanimate, I'm willing, not a slave.
This meditation, now complete, my consciousness does save;
my corporeal self, serene, now bonded, leaves the cave.

Notes

PARENTING

Our children die a thousand deaths,
but other mammals, one,
for parents yearn for bygone times
ere childhood days are done.

We watch our children grow and learn,
are proud but saddened, too;
once curious, naive, and dear;
the loss of these we rue.

We teach them lessons, guide their lives,
which starts a wistful flood
of thoughts nostalgic that we feel
about our flesh and blood.

These memories remind us that
our children's youth must end,
to be replaced by grown-up souls,
adults we need not tend.

But mammals never mark the dates
their offspring grow, mature.
Their young live life until they die,
a mass of flesh and fur.

*N*otes

Secondaries
  The inner flight feathers that run along but perpendicular
  to a bird's 'arm.'

Primaries
  Elongated outer flight feathers, the 'fingertip feathers.'

FLYING

Aerodynamic shape of wings
helps birds stay in the air

while soaring or in powered flight,
wings working as a pair.

The secondaries of a bird
give wings their shape and lift,

while thrust comes from the primaries
to make bird's flying swift.

The way in which birds ply their wings
Determines path of flight

How much, how hard their pinions move
affects the flying height.

Bald eagles can do barrel rolls,
Ospreys dive feet first,

Hummers aim for nectar tubes
To quench their nagging thirst.

Kingfishers plunge from branch for fish
Crows 'row' their wings to fly

Male woodcocks zig-zag up and up
then tumble from the sky.

*N*otes

Polymer
   Chemical compound with long molecules.

Gossamer
   Filaments from a web spun by a spider.

SPIDER WEBS

All spider types make protein silk, as liquid, pure and clear,
then load it in their spinnerets, the structures on their rear.

The polymer extruded firms as strong and tough as nails,
yet flexible, with tensile strength, the gossamer-made rails.

The architect first takes a chance, throws caution to the wind,
Letting go a test balloon with end of tether pinned.

The silk balloon, made sticky first, floats off on gentle breeze;
balloon adheres to leaf or twig, is tightened then with ease.

Back and forth across the bridge to strengthen and inspect.
From anchor points, the frame is built in plane that stands erect.

First, central hub then radii are strung with silky strands.
Orb weavers next the spirals make, with tiny hook-like hands:

the dry lines first, from inside out, so spiders don't get caught,
then "capture spirals," outside in, with spider glue are fraught.

Orb weaver species make their webs in every shape and size.
Their beauty makes us marvel at the engineering prize.

So lovely and so intricate, it's hard for human thought
to fathom spiders' silk reuse; they eat what they have wrought.

Notes

Happed
 Happened by chance.

TREE FALL

I led our fleet that gifted day
along the river's shore.
Our canoes divided water,
my vessel in the fore.
As was my wont, I talked a while
before we paddled more.
'Tween islands lush we moved our boats
as many times before.
But this time came a thing so rare,
it added to my lore.
I knew not what would happen
nor what was for us in store.

This common, rarely-seen event
happed with no human hand:
the oldest tree before our eyes
fell over to the land.

$\mathcal{N}$otes

Sallying
  The hunting technique in which
  birds fly out from a branch,
  nab an insect out of the air,
  and return to the branch,
  also called hawking.

WHO SAID I DIDN'T GO?

The air was fresh, the breezes light,
the grass had dotted dew.

The Sun began to warm the Earth,
the sky turned brilliant blue.

While hiking we saw many birds,
I named each one in turn.

The songs and calls of birds we saw
were next for them to learn.

I noted bill diversity
that matched the way they ate:

a cone-shaped cracker, sipping straw,
and chisel for a trait.

Two rivals hunted same resource,
each living by its tally.

The swallows caught bugs on the wing,
the pewees caught by sally.

With unlike feeding styles, the birds
stayed out of other's way.

They taught us how they share the wealth
while eating insect prey.

We saw more birds that blessed hike
and heard a Sunday crow.

When hikers talked of church, one said,
"Who said I didn't go?"

Notes

Forb
   An herbaceous (non-woody) flowering plant that is
   not grass-like, but often grows alongside of grasses

A SURPRISE

Toward colors of the forb I crept, to photograph the bloom
with flowers' petals woven low in Mother Nature's loom.

For land ne'er touched by human hands, nor sprinkler, nor mower,
I wanted level nature shot, so knelt down even lower.

But when too close to Earth I leaned, a milk snake buzzed its tail
in driest leaves to scare me off. In that it did not fail.

I knew it was not rattlesnake, but that was just my smarts.
I yelped and fled from unseen snake as told by heart of hearts.

*N*otes

Badger Camper
   One who attends Wisconsin Badger Camp,
   a recreational camp for persons of all abilities.

Hale
   Strong and healthy, hearty

ANOTHER SURPRISE

Each week I'd lead a hike or two or three
at camp for those with disability.
The Badger Campers followed me on trail,
we slowed the pace if someone was not hale.

I stopped the hike when something made a sound,
Could not mistake this rattle from the ground.

"We must go back. A big tree blocks our way,"
a counsellor, quick-witted, thought to say,

This cleared the path before the snake could strike.
Without the snake, we finished off our hike.

Notes

The poem refers to the British nursery rhyme
about magpies that predicts the future, depending
how many magpies are present. It begins,
"One for sorrow, two for joy...."

A CHANCE ENCOUNTER

One morn while walking down a London street,
Bird-watching couple did I chance to meet.

They wished to catch and join a larger group,
with experts, we would follow on a loop.

I learned the European robin's song,
with perky notes, some buzzy, kind of long.

So many birds, I seemed a little boy
just learning magpies' sorrow and their joy.

A joy of friendship came to me that day
like artwork chalked upon the pavement grey.

I called them later, asked if they were free
next day or after for a cuppa (tea).

Mostly, I'm timid and not very brave,
Except if others would want Earth to save.

We dwellers of Earth, should take a long view
and give Earth all the respect that She's due.

Notes

BULLLHEAD FISHING

I was never fond of fishing, not walleye, perch, or bass,
or any fish caught from a boat; I'd want my feet on grass.

The only kind of fish I'd catch were sunfish in the sun,
we'd use for bait so chopped them up, before the day was done.

Emerging later, 'fore the dark, to set the lines we'd tend,
each cousin watching poles at hand until the very end.

Once poles were set, we'd go about the business of the night,
we'd check the poles for bait-less lines or bobbers out of sight.

Then, best of all, between the checks, were cards and cards and cards.
We bet no money, just had fun, no need for any guards.

The cards were conservation ploy to think about the lake,
and bottom-dwelling fish therein, precautions that we'd take.

With "whiskers" soft a bullhead feels what passes by its head,
but spines near fins are hard and sharp, may injure you instead.

Low oxygen and turbid pools are bullhead habitat,
they'd likely choose another place, but no one asked them that.

Notes

A MOMENT WITH GRANDMA

While I was young, came Grandma to our door.
She'd visit us a week, or even more.

With Dad, she spoke Croatian for her lore,
We nodded at her many days of yore.

And then one day outside was something new.
She ope'd the curtains for a better view.

There framed a picture of uncounted birds,
narrated by her best Croatian words.

From one horizon to the other flew,
in speckled sky that otherwise was blue,

enormous flock of birds, all colored black,
a million minds all on a single track,

wherein no thoughts of territories grew,
migration, only, as the blackbirds flew.

For next half hour, Grandma bit her tongue,
and in that moment, all who watched were young.

Notes

JACOB'S LADDER

Rare evenings are with spirit filled,
the excess gives us light
With beams to build our dreams at times
to make our spirits bright.
Some see the ladder, heaven-aimed,
that Jacob dreamed one night.
Still others see the Buddha Rays
through fingers almost tight.

But science notes just scattering
by particles and haze
Arriving near the setting sun
and stimulating praise,
this spirit light unusual
appears and briefly stays
inviting us to grapple with
God's scientific ways.

Notes

MAPS

If drawn out on a paper sheet or cast upon a screen,
the data has been published there for anyone to glean.

The key unlocks the symbols that describe Earth for the keen.
They lead us from our comfort zone to many sights unseen.

The scale determines useful size, to carry and to see.
When scale is large, big things look small and smaller things look wee.

The value of an inset map, where crucial details be,
important things of smaller size, seems obvious to me.

The magic of a map is found in neither key nor scale.
The very essence of a map from head to end of tail

transposes actuality of every hill and dale
from 3D down to two and back with ne'er in mind a fail.

Notes

Hie
    Hurry

SALAMANDER

While camping on a trip alone in tranquil part of state,
I pitched my tent near gentle stream, the fire would have to wait.

Flowing water soothed my ears, so full from noise that day.
Some crickets chirped, grasshoppers buzzed, but water found sleep's way.

Then Dawn began to inundate the darkness of the sky.
I grabbed the flap but slowed my pace, no reason yet to hie.

Unzipping slowly as I could, revealed a hidden sight,
a spotted salamander near, its visit a delight.

It stood stock still, quiescently, not hidden by the dark.
So common yet so rarely seen, this denizen of park.

It left no sign of movement there; no tiny mark on trail.
A short time on, it had not stepped, nor even flicked its tail.

I watched much longer, mesmerized, it did not stir or flee.
Until, at last, I made a noise, it left and set us free.

The herp, from its biology of motionless defense;
me, from waning wonderment that still held me in suspense.

Notes

NATURAL HISTORY

Our fam'ly owned some hillside land, its acres numbered ten.
We didn't live too far away, I biked there now and then.

With grass aplenty, mostly brome, there wasn't much to see
of native plants or what's entailed in nat'ral history.

In storm one year tornadic winds took out an aged oak.
My father and his friend next morn cut all before I woke.

"Please let me count that red oak's rings before you haul away."
One hundred thirty-six I got, with checks it did not sway.

The count reflected age at death, enabled me to try
to understand what lived nearby and grew beneath the sky.

The point on Earth the tree would sprout was near a settlement,
the second in Wisconsin-land, where many Norsemen went.

The tree we'd cut, not yet a seed, would grow with oaks of white,
and in the shade of older trees, where sunshine not as bright.

In eighteen hundred thirty-nine, some took their land for free,
replacing nearby village of the Potawatomi.

In middle of the century, once cholera had struck,
'twas named the Town of Norway and ancestral name has stuck.

The tree was not susceptible to cholera or flu,
so there, above Wind Lake by name, the stalwart red oak grew

until my father owned the land where history was writ
in ev'ry leaf of ev'ry tree, so learning never quit.

For hundred plus three dozen years it held its secrets well.
I read its years at end of life, no spring-times still to tell.

*N*otes

Hera *(HAIR-uh)*
   The Greek goddess Hera
   was renamed Juno by the Romans.

Heracles *(HAIR-uh-klees)*
   The Greek hero Heracles
   was renamed Hercules by the Romans.

MILKY WAY

Our galaxy was named by Greeks from legendary tale,
when Hera, nursing Heracles lost milk in glowing trail.

Astronomers in ancient times, as Hera felt dismay,
looked up to hazy patch in sky and named it "Milky Way."

They saw not hundred billion lights nor spiral arms nor bars.
From Earth, can't see Way's blackest hole, just forests of its stars.

The nearby stars as trees are seen, some up, some down, ahead.
For distant stars, not each is seen, galactic glow instead.

The far-off trees give edge-on view, green stripe upon the land.
In darkened skies on cloudless nights, the galaxy's a band.

While pondering black holes and Time, or tree-lines in a park,
we may begin to understand, but find we're in the dark.

Ion *("EYE-on")*
> An atom or group of atoms that has
> lost or gained one or more electrons.

Radiant
> The point in the heavens from which
> meteors appear to originate.

METEORS

Earth's orbit intercepts the path
left by a comet's tail,

whose rock, dust, ice, and ion gas
produce a glowing trail

when entering Earth's atmosphere,
where they encounter drag

that lights the speeding molecules,
stressed by the ones that lag.

The streaks of light ephemeral
bedazzle conscious mind,

but focusing a moment late
frustrates one as if blind.

Ubiquitous, yet personal,
radiant are the showers.

Shared glimpses of a falling star
are deeper felt than flowers.

Notes

Accrete
Increase in size by a series of additions.

Penumbra *("pee-NUM-bra")*
The part of the shadow of Earth or the
Moon in which all sunlight is not blocked

Umbra
The part of the shadow of Earth or the
Moon in which all sunlight is blocked

Maria *("MAH-ree-uh")*
The "seas" found on the moon, which are flat, dark plains.

Sol *("sole")*
Our Sun.

Baily's Beads
The "beads" of sunlight shining between the
moon's mountains when a solar eclipse is near totality,
first explained exactly by Francis Baily in 1836.

Shadow bands
Undulating wavy bands of light and dark shone
on plain, light-colored surfaces just before and
after a total solar eclipse.

ECLIPSES

Cooling gas and dust in space
did long ago accrete
to form the planets 'round the Sun
and make the Earth complete.

The Moon was formed at later time,
its orbit an ellipse,
and, when aligned with Earth and Sun,
occasions an eclipse.

Lunar

First seen is faint penumbra
of copper-colored light,
followed by Earth's silhouette,
the umbra, black as night.

Earth's shadow, cast upon full Moon,
creeps 'cross the lunar face,
extinguishing the maria,
which vanish in black space.

Solar

The unseen orb of newest Moon
eclipses solar light;
when totally obscuring Sol,
it turns the day to night.

Moon's mountains Baily's Beads create
along the crescent Sun.
Rare shadow bands of light and dark,
appear and then are done.

Notes

Fusing
   The process of nuclear fusion

Supernova
   A star that is exploding

Sol *("sole")*
   Our Sun

SUN

Within the furnace at its core,
our Sun does elemental chore

by fusing hydrogen to form
new helium in plasma storm.

Exploding forge will atoms bake,
to carbon and some others make.

Most heavy elements arise
with supernova stars' demise.

But not our Sun, its greatest grace
is radiation sent through space,

that powers weather, growth of plants,
affecting fauna's living chance,

providing and withdrawing Life,
the touch of Sun on Earth is rife.

In nightly dark, there is no Sol,
yet everywhere is solar role.

Notes

Corn
    The main grain of a country or region.

Perigee *("PARE-i-jee")*
    The point in Earth's orbit around the Sun at which
    Earth is closest to the Sun (sometime in December)

Names in ALL CAPS are traditional
Algonquin names for full moons.

Names in **bold** come from traditions
and cultures other than Algonquin.

The Harvest Moon is not part of the monthly cycle
of full moons because it is the full moon nearest to the
Autumnal Equinox so can occur in September or October.

FULL MOONS

A spirit WOLF howls from the ages of **old**,
Full Moon after Yule with its treasures and gold.

When SNOW causes **hunger**, the moon never blue,
but may lack the "full" phase, opposing the new.

New WORMs work the soil and are eaten by **crow**s,
with **Lenten** snow **crust**y, sweet maple **sap** flows.

Moss PINKs highlight **sprouting grass** growing so new.
Fish easy to catch and the robins' **egg**s blue.

More FLOWERs in May ease the **corn-planting** toil;
weeds eaten by cows add nutrition to soil.

Wild STRAWBERRYs flourish in **hot** moon of June,
in Europe it's **rose**s that see the same moon.

BUCKs' antlers encased in soft velvet to show
and under the **thunder**, the **hay** stacks do grow.

The ancient fish, STURGEON, is easily speared;
when, **grain**, **hay**, and the **green corn** can be reared

CORN moon in September is not always maize,
main grain may be **barley** that livestock don't graze.

The HUNTER sees hunted in light of the night,
first **blood** then there's movement, tries not to lose sight.

A BEAVER cuts **frosty** trees, making a dome,
with offspring for helpers, the dome becomes home.

The COLD MOON reflected in long winter nights,
this perigee moon is the greatest of sights.

Notes

Epicycles
   Circles imagined along planets' orbits that helped
   to describe observations better mathematically.

Ptolemy is pronounced with a silent "P."

For this poem, Tycho Brahe's name is pronounced
as my professor pronounced it, *"tee-koh brah-hay."*

THE HEAVENS

Sumerians, Akkadians, four thousand years ago,
Looked up and saw in pitch black skies a starlit picture show.

As Taurus, Leo, Scorpio, and Capricorn first cast,
did usher in the seasons four and told of stories past.

The cycle of their zodiac, which moved around the sky,
was passed along to ancient Greeks, with explanation bye.

So Aristotle placed the stars and planets that were known
upon concentric crystal spheres, themselves were never shown.

With epicycles, Ptolemy explained how planets moved;
For more than fourteen hundred years he could not be disproved.

Then Tycho Brahe smashed the orbs and epicycles, too.
The planets traced elliptic arcs, Johannes Kepler knew.

They moved around the Sun, not Earth, Copernicus was sure.
In Galileo's telescope were moons of Jupiter.

The telescope that Hubble dreamed was built by modern tech,
but based on bygone scientists and answered to their beck.

Notes

The words in **bold print** (and many more)
are freshwater mussels of the Upper Mississippi River

The name, Lilliput, for this tiny mussel, comes from
the name of the island of Lilliput in Jonathan Swift's book,
Gulliver's Travels, where all the inhabitants were very small.

Pistol Grips
    a.k.a. Buckhorn mussels

MUSSELTOWN

The clams I've seen in Mussel Town left stories in my mind
of characters from olden times in shells that we could find.

The shells I wanted most to miss and avoid Achilles' fate
were **heelsplitters, creek** and **white**, though cutting power not great.

I traveled next with Gulliver and searched for tiny **Lilliput**
by land and sea and ev'ry where that I could go by foot.

Lenses from my **spectacle case** made it easier to see,
but if I used some **snuffbox** snuff, I might then over-see.

That night we lay in **mucket** bed and got so full of muck,
We used a **washboard** for our clothes, so didn't have to chuck.

I had not a **fat pocketbook, no floaters, strange** or **flat.**
Our **papershells** were **fragile**-named, but strong in spite of that.

I asked my fellow traveler for someplace we could go
where we could spend the whole long day with not a lot of dough.

The character said "zoo" for sure, then later, maybe, "feet."
and there it was, between my toes, a laminated sheet,

a guide to river mussel shells' menagerie of names,
not quite a zoo, but close enough to what the story claims.

Fawnfoot, Deertoe, Elktoe, too,
Buckhorn, Bullhead, more for you.

Elephant Ear with **Monkey Face**,
a **pigtoe** seems not out of place.

*N*otes

Serotonin
  The brain chemical that in humans determines mood,
  but in locusts, triggers swarming behavior

TWO TALES OF A GRASSHOPPER

Grasshoppers of the short-horned kind
near Earth on grassy plants are found,
to eat the food, politely dined,
but not yet any dregs around.
If arid lands the rains do sate
they grow green plants most everywhere
then feasting comes and seals their fate,
till not a plant is anywhere.
Some 'hoppers into locusts turned
by serotonin held within
that powers frenzy till adjourned
to make a raucous chewing din.
But, worst of all, when locusts touch,
which, in a swarm, they can't avoid.
In parts of world, they're hated much,
but in US, we're just annoyed.

Notes

MR. SALTZMANN'S GARDEN

On sunny days, we used to walk the hundred feet or so
to Mr. Saltzmann's garden shack, Mom rarely told us, "No."
We never went inside his shack, he said not, "Yes, you may."
His hand pump, though, was free to use, we drank from it each day.
The garden, one full acre large, was where he grew his crop,
raspberry plants in such long rows, they never seemed to stop.
He labored hard, but took a break whenever we appeared.
We never ate his berries, though, the produce that he reared.
Just four was I, my sister, five, when first we went next door,
where all we ever did was talk and started not a chore.
I've pondered what we talked about, but don't remember what
the details, even subjects were, by Mr. Saltzmann's hut.
He planted in the spring each year, so reaped on summer days
and weeded when he got the chance, with rarely time to laze.

One year in latter summertime, my father said one day,
"Let's go see Mr. Saltzmann now, he lives not far away."
Dad buttoned up a button-down, Mom donned her favorite blouse,
five minutes' drive, Dad parked the car at Mr. Saltzmann's house.
He greeted us outside his home and introduced his wife.
We looked inside their living space and saw his other life.
She wore a simple dress she sewed and he a bolo tie.
With all the fancy things about, I suddenly was shy:
I didn't want to break their things, so hid behind Mom's skirt
and didn't touch the crystalware, I brushed, instead, my shirt.
the pieces of fine furniture, alone or matched in sets,
the tables, lamps, and carpeting, the fancy cabinets.
One cabinet held curios, which fascinated me
Although we looked until we left, I wanted more to see.

He never showed his house again, nor sat outside his shack,
for he was in his 80s then, soon after, life went black.
His words are long-forgotten now, his actions are my guide:
When interrupted, take a break, hard work will give you pride

Notes

About the Author

The scientifically romantic nature poetry of Paul Košir has its academic roots in his nine years as a student at the University of Wisconsin-Madison. There he earned bachelor's degrees in math, natural science, and history. In 2010 he received a master's degree in natural resources and environmental education from UW-Stevens Point.

The experiential poetry was drawn mostly from his twelve years as the naturalist at Wyalusing State Park near Prairie du Chien, Wisconsin. He also drew on this background to write articles for *Wisconsin Natural Resources* and *La Crosse Magazine* and to publish the book, Wyalusing History.

Košir has taught biology, physical science, and math at the high school level and earth science, biology, and environmental issues at the college level. As a naturalist, he taught all ages about nature through hikes, programs, and displays, something he still does occasionally as a volunteer.

Born in Milwaukee, Košir now lives in La Crosse with his wife and their two sons. He enjoys writing, hiking, bird-watching, gardening, traveling, and visiting relatives.

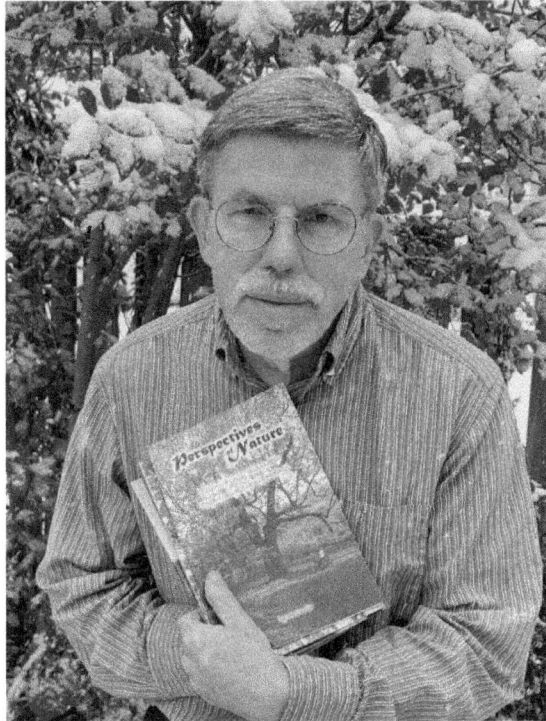

Notes

Also by this author:

Perspectives of Nature

Perspectives of Nature Volume 2

Perspectives of Nature Volume 3

Perspectives of Nature Volume 4

www.ingramcontent.com/pod-product-compliance
Lightning Source LLC
Chambersburg PA
CBHW052116030426
42335CB00025B/3005